Theater Actors
Then and Now

Kathleen C. Null Petersen

Contributing Author
Emily R. Smith, M.A.Ed.

Associate Editor
Christina Hill, M.A.

Assistant Editor
Torrey Maloof

Editorial Director
Emily R. Smith, M.A.Ed.

Project Researcher
Gillian Eve Makepeace

Editor-in-Chief
Sharon Coan, M.S.Ed.

Editorial Manager
Gisela Lee, M.A.

Creative Director
Lee Aucoin

Illustration Manager
Timothy J. Bradley

Designers
Lesley Palmer
Debora Brown
Zac Calbert
Robin Erickson

Project Consultant
Corinne Burton, M.A.Ed.

Publisher
Rachelle Cracchiolo, M.S.Ed.

Teacher Created Materials Publishing

5301 Oceanus Drive
Huntington Beach, CA 92649
http://www.tcmpub.com
ISBN 978-0-7439-9379-1

Table of Contents

Acting Across Time

Have you ever seen a play? The men and women on the stage are called **actors**. Their job is to act like the characters in a story. Plays can be funny or sad. There are even some plays that have lots of music. These are called **musicals** or **operas** (AH-pruhz).

Acting has been around for more than 2,500 years! The first actor was a man who lived in **ancient** (AYN-shunt) Greece. He wrote a play for a special contest. His play won the contest. And, this is where theater got its start.

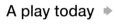 An ancient Greek theater

Actors in a funny
Greek play

A play today ➧

Ancient Actors

The ancient Greeks were the first actors. Greek acting was very different than acting today. At first, there was only one actor on stage. He said all his lines to the **audience** (AU-dee-uhntz). Later, Greek plays had two or three actors. These actors talked to each other. The plays also had a **chorus** (KOR-uhs). They sang songs or told important parts of the story.

▼ The chorus from a Greek play

Greek actors wore large masks. The masks had big open mouths. The actors had to yell their lines. They used big movements with their bodies to show action. The ancient Romans also had plays. Their plays had many actors. The Romans used more props and scenery (SEEN-er-ree), too.

▲ Greek mask

Funny or Sad?

Greek plays can be **comedies** or **tragedies** (TRAJ-uh-dees). A comedy is a play that is funny. The audience enjoys the play because it makes them laugh. A tragedy is exciting to watch. You never know what is going to happen next.

▲ Two Greek actors carved on a stone wall

Acting Changes with Time

In the year 475, a new time period began. It was called the **Middle Ages**. Church leaders controlled many things. They did not allow any plays.

At that time, most people did not understand what was going on in church. The services were in **Latin**. Most people did not speak Latin. So, the church leaders started to create plays. These plays shared Bible stories. This helped people understand church better.

Jugglers

Some actors worked even when plays were not allowed. These men and women were street performers. That means they juggled, sang, or danced on the streets. People paid them to perform.

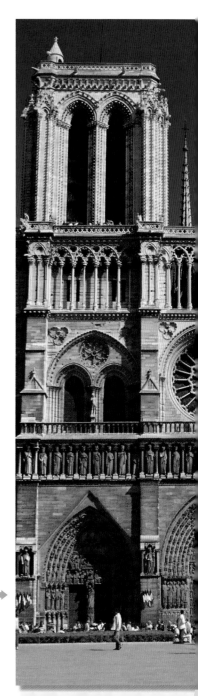

The Notre Dame Cathedral ➡ was built in the Middle Ages.

Soon, people started writing plays again. But, not all of these were about the Bible. So, these playwrights (PLAY-rites) had to be careful. They could get in trouble for writing these new plays.

⬆ This scene is from a village play from long ago.

William Shakespeare

Christopher Marlowe

The Rebirth of Acting

In the year 1350, the world started to change. Theaters began to open. Actors could be in plays, and they would not get in trouble.

A man named William Shakespeare wrote many plays. His plays had lots of actors and great action. The plays were performed in England. People still read his plays today.

The Rose was a famous theater in London. Many well-known people acted there. Some of Shakespeare's plays were seen there. Another English playwright was Christopher Marlowe. His plays were also performed at The Rose.

The Renaissance

The years after the Middle Ages were called the **Renaissance** (reh-nuh-SAUNTZ). The world changed. People wanted to learn more. They began to read poetry and plays. And, more people began to write. Art and music were popular once again.

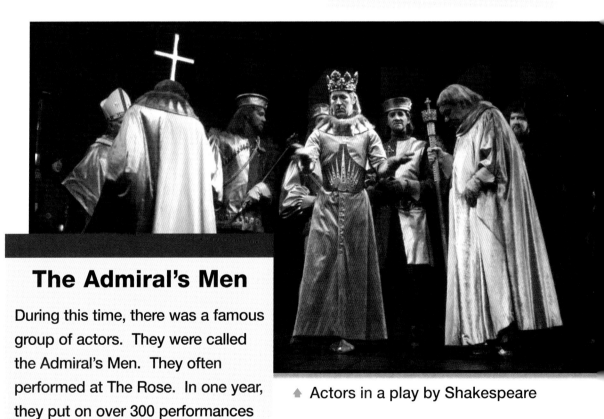

The Admiral's Men

During this time, there was a famous group of actors. They were called the Admiral's Men. They often performed at The Rose. In one year, they put on over 300 performances (puhr-FOR-muhntz-iz)!

⬆ Actors in a play by Shakespeare

Theaters

Greeks saw plays in **theaters** that were built into the sides of hills. These theaters were called **amphitheaters** (AM-fuh-thee-uh-tuhrz). It was hard to see the actors from so far away.

▲ Greek amphitheater

In England, the theaters had no roofs. So, rain and sun could come in during plays. And, the audience was very close to the stage.

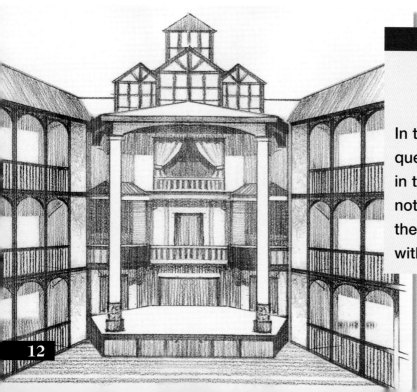

How About a Roof?

In the 1600s, kings and queens went to see plays in the theaters. They did not want to get wet. So, theaters were soon built with roofs.

◀ This is an open theater from long ago. It did not have a roof.

Later, people in Italy began to use a new kind of stage. It looked like a picture frame. It was inside a building. The audience sat away from the stage. These stages were more like the stages in theaters today.

Let There Be Light!

Theaters became more popular when the lighting got better. The audience liked being able to really see the actors. Gaslights were used first. Then, theaters used electricity.

⬆ Theater light

The new stages made it easy to change scenes. There were many special effects. And, costumes became more realistic (REE-uhl-is-tik).

⬆ This theater was built in 1890.

Theater Acting in the United States

People came from Europe (YUR-uhp) to colonial America. They loved plays. So, they built theaters. Many plays were performed in Boston.

There is a special kind of play called a **melodrama** (MEL-uh-drahm-uh). It is so **dramatic** (druh-MAT-ik) that it is funny. It is a bit crazy, too. Melodramas were popular in the United States.

▲ An American melodrama from 1916

New York City

People from everywhere in the world travel to New York City. They go there to see plays on Broadway. The theaters there are large. And, the plays are very exciting.

▲ A poster for a play in 1927

In the 1900s, people started to go to movies. They stopped seeing plays. So, theaters started to close. Many people worked hard to keep some theaters open. It worked! Soon, plays became popular again. Today, there are thousands of community theaters around the country.

Have Theater, Will Travel

How would you like to travel around the world? That is what the Missoula Children's Theatre does every year. They go to all 50 states and at least 12 other countries.

↟ This is a theater in France in 1830.

Theaters Across Europe

Theater is still very popular all over the world. There are theaters in every country. Some theaters are famous because they are **unique** (you-NEEK).

In 1887, an actor opened a theater in France. He used his mother's furniture for plays. He wanted the sets to look real.

There was a really interesting play in Italy once. It was about Aesop's Fables. The stage had real caves. Over 300 kinds of animals were in the play!

The Abbey Theatre is a famous theater in Ireland. It sits on a cement raft next to a river. Many plays by Irish writers can be seen there.

⬆ This is the symbol for the Abbey Theatre.

Part of the Show

In Spain, there is a theater called La Carnicería Teatro (kar-nee-seh-REE-uh teh-AH-troh). It is a **modern** theater that shows fun plays. If you see a play there, you might end up on stage as part of the show.

◀ Poster about a play in 1894

Acting in Asia

In Vietnam, the *cheo* (CHAY-oh) is a popular play. It only has three actors. There is a hero or a good man. There is a heroine or a good woman. And, there is a clown. People love this type of play.

▲ Theater in China in the 1700s

Kabuki (kuh-BOO-kee) is a special Japanese play. Men play all the parts. *Kabuki* is very melodramatic. But, the stories are about history. Some *kabuki* plays are very well known. They've been around for hundreds of years.

The *zaju* (ZAH-ju) are famous Chinese plays. They are very old. Most of them are love stories. Women acted in these plays. That is different than most other countries. Usually, women were not allowed to act.

A Puppet Show on the River

In Vietnam, people put on interesting puppet shows in water. They stand in water up to their waists. The surface of the water is the stage.

Two actors in a Japanese play. One actor is dressed as a lion.

Theater Directors

Besides actors, plays have **directors** (duh-REK-tuhrz). They tell the actors what to do.

Kathy Busby directs at the Orange County Children's Theatre. She says that it is "exciting to see words on a page come to life through an actor." She has loved theater since she was a little girl. She used to make books into plays. Her friends would put on the plays in her garage.

Ms. Busby says that seeing real actors is magical. You do not have that at a movie or on television.

This theater will soon be filled with a big audience.

William Shakespeare performs for Queen Elizabeth.

Shakespeare

People know that William Shakespeare wrote a lot of plays. But, did you know that he was an actor and a director? And, he was even a poet!

The World of Theater Actors

Theater is found all around the world. It is a popular place to go. Not even television shows or movies have stopped people from putting on plays.

▼ These actors are performing in a play.

▲ An audience at an opera house

People love to see plays on stage. Actors would not have jobs without the audience. Actors love to make people happy by putting on plays. Theaters have been around since ancient times. And, they will still be around for many years to come.

A Day in the Life Then

Richard Burbage (1567–1619)

Richard Burbage (RIH-churd BER-behj) was an actor in England. He lived a long time ago. He acted in many plays. But, he is most famous for acting in plays by William Shakespeare. Mr. Burbage played the main part in many plays. He loved the theater. He even helped build a famous playhouse called The Globe Theatre.

Let's pretend to ask Richard Burbage some questions about his job.

Why did you decide to be an actor?

My father was an actor. My brother is also an actor. I cannot imagine having any other job. I have been acting ever since I was a child. It is my favorite thing to do.

What is your day like?

Right now I am acting in a play called *Hamlet*. It is a tragedy. My friend William Shakespeare wrote it. I play the main part. Every day I wake up and work to memorize my lines. Then, we meet at the theater and practice.

What do you like most about your job?

I love to act in front of an audience. The opening night of a play is always the best. It is so exciting!

▼ This is the new Globe Theatre. It was rebuilt to look like the original theater.

Tools of the Trade Then

This was a playbill. It was a small poster that described a play. Playbills let people know when and where a play was being performed. They are still used today.

Long ago, theater actors used to wear masks. Now, most actors use makeup.

Another tool for actors was the theater itself. And, they also needed the audience! Actors needed people to come to their plays.

Tools of the Trade Now

Long ago, stages were lit by sunlight. If a play was at night, they used candlelight. Today, theaters have stage lights in many colors.

Theaters today can be very big. Microphones (my-kruh-FOHNS) are used on the stage. That way, people sitting in the back of the theater can hear.

Today, most theaters are inside. That way, a play can go on even if it rains or snows outside.

A Day in the Life Now

Caryn Miller

Caryn Miller is a college student. She is studying to be a theater actor. At school she takes many classes about theater. Her favorite play is *Ragtime*. She saw it on Broadway.

Why did you decide to become a theater actor?

I have always loved acting. I have been acting ever since I was young. I used to put on pretend plays for my family. When I was in high school, I acted in a play called *Annie*. I loved it. That is when I decided to study acting in college.

What is your day like?

Right now I am in school a lot. But, I am also in a play. It is a play by Shakespeare called

A Midsummer Night's Dream.
I play a fairy.

I get to perform in shows on the weekends. I look forward to it all week long!

What do you like most about acting?

Theater acting is exciting. It is so fun to dress up and be on stage. I love being in costume. But, I also like that I learn something new with every play. It is great that audiences still love to watch Shakespeare's plays after all these years!

⬆ This is Ms. Miller wearing her costume for *A Midsummer Night's Dream*.

This is the outdoor ➡ theater where Ms. Miller performs.

Glossary

actors—people who perform in plays, movies, or television shows

amphitheaters—round or oval theaters without roofs that have seats cut into the hillsides

ancient—from a long time ago

audience—a group of people who watch something

chorus—a group of actors who sing or speak together

comedies—plays or films that are funny

directors—people in charge of the actions and details of plays

dramatic—exciting and lively

Latin—the language spoken by ancient Romans

melodrama—play with a dramatic plot and exaggerated action

Middle Ages—period in European history before the Renaissance (475–1500)

modern—happening now, new

musicals—plays with singing and dancing

operas—plays with singing instead of talking

Renaissance—a period of history when there was a growth in the arts and culture

theaters—buildings where people can watch plays and movies

tragedies—plays that are sad and dramatic

unique—one of a kind

Index

Credits

Acknowledgements

Special thanks to Caryn Miller for providing the *Day in the Life Now* interview. Ms. Miller is currently a student at California State University, Long Beach.

Image Credits

front cover Corel; p.1 Corel; p.4 Corel; p.5 (top) The Granger Collection, New York; p.5 (bottom) Corel; p.6 Corel; p.7 (left) Jim Steinhart/travelphotobase.com; p.7 (right) The Granger Collection, New York; pp.8–9 Corbis; p.9 The Granger Collection, New York; p.10 (left) The Granger Collection, New York; p.10 (right) The Granger Collection, New York; p.11 Corel; p.12 (top) iStockphoto.com/Alec Runge; p.12 (bottom) Courtesy of Emily Smith; p.13 (top) Hemera Technologies, Inc.; p.13 (bottom) Denver Public Library; p.14 The Granger Collection, New York; p.15 The Granger Collection, New York; p.16 The Granger Collection, New York; p.17 (left) The Granger Collection, New York; p.17 (right) The Granger Collection, New York; p.18 The Granger Collection, New York; p.19 The Library of Congress; pp.20–21 Garret Bautista/Shutterstock, Inc.; p.21 The Library of Congress; p.22 Corel; p.23 Izim M. Gulcuk/Shutterstock, Inc.; p.24 Hulton Archive/Getty Images; p.25 Lance Bellers/Shutterstock, Inc.; p.26 (top right) Tiburon Studios/Shutterstock, Inc.; p.26 (top left) The Library of Congress; p.26 (bottom) The Library of Congress; p.27 (top) Shannon West/Shutterstock, Inc.; p.27 (middle) Steve Mann/Shutterstock, Inc.; p.27 (bottom) Tad Denson/Shutterstock, Inc.; p.28 Courtesy of Peter Pulido; p.29 (top) Courtesy of Peter Pulido; p.29 (bottom) Courtesy of Peter Pulido; back cover The Library of Congress